SEVEN

SEVEN

SEVEN

HOW I RAISED MY SEVEN CHILDREN

FRANCES HART

ARCHWAY
PUBLISHING

Archway Publishing books may be ordered through booksellers or by contacting:

Archway Publishing
1663 Liberty Drive
Bloomington, IN 47403
www.archwaypublishing.com
844-669-3957

ISBN: 978-1-6657-6237-3 (sc)
ISBN: 978-1-6657-6238-0 (hc)
ISBN: 978-1-6657-6239-7 (e)

Library of Congress Control Number: 2024913517

Print information available on the last page.

Archway Publishing rev. date: 09/06/2024

This book is dedicated to my eleven grandchildren: Meghan, Matthew, Elijah, Reana, Analisa, Robert, Anyah, Piper, Temple, Blake, Roman

And Seven Children

They are kind, caring, strong, consistent, and loving.

CONTENTS

WHEN I WAS 5 years old, I did not realize what I did as a child and the things my mother instilled in me became a part of who I am and someday will determine what I will do in the future. There are many things I enjoyed as a child and strived to do that helped me in raising my children.

I lived with my mom, twin sister, grandma, and uncle. We had a routine of how we did things from morning until night. I was five years old and I kept that way of doing things until I was eighteen. We went to church on Sundays. I loved going to church. I enjoyed listening to the choir sing and I liked playing with the children after church.

My family celebrated all the season holidays, especially Christmas, Thanksgiving, and Easter. We also celebrated birthdays with our family. We went on summer vacation when school was out. We traveled to Houston and Ennis Texas every year. My sister and I would stay in Houston for two weeks with my older sister. Then, we would go to Ennis and stay with my aunt and uncle for two weeks.

When my older sister moved to Dallas Texas, we visited her for longer periods of time.

Although, there was a routine in doing things, there is some dark side to my childhood story. I was extremely poor, I do remember eating every day, however, we had to share the food. When my mom prepared fried chicken, my sister and I had to share eating the chicken breast. I would eat the chicken breast for one serving and she would eat it for the next serving. We had enough food but not an abundance of food, clothing, and other necessities that people enjoyed.

THINGS NEEDED TO BE SUCCESSFUL IN RAISING SEVEN CHILDREN

FIRST FIND THE passion in each child. You must work hard to obtain success. Never give up on yourself and your children. You will need positive character traits to be successful in raising children. You must have traits like honesty,bravery, strength, consistency,caring, and loving. You must believe you can accomplished these things. All things that you think you cannot accomplish will be within reach. Think positive even when you have those negative thoughts on your mind. Keep the faith. The Lord will see you through whatever troubles you may have. If you do not believe in Jesus Christ, then, believe in yourself and think positive. Remember when caring for your children, take care of needs first, then take care of wants. Help your children in their efforts to succeed in becoming adults then still support them in adulthood. You will know when you have done your best. Your adult children will succeed.

You raised your kids like yourself.

I received positive treatment from my mom when I was growing up. Mom taught positive traits like being kind to others. She cared for my sister and me. She raised us in an incredibly positive way so raising children became easy. When I taught my children to be kind, I demonstrated what kindness looked like from my mom's teachings. One way of being kind is giving a helping hand to someone in need. Mom's teachings of being grateful, caring, and kind had a profound effect on my success in raising my children.

MY OUTCOME AND RESEARCH

WHEN YOU TALK about raising seven children, people want to know what you did. So, I am going to tell you some of the things I did in raising my seven children. First, I used positive reinforcement when they were behaving inappropriately. When I gave a command of what you must not do, they did not follow. I would redirect that behavior to something positive. For example, I said "No TV for tonight, because you are not doing homework, if they start to do the homework, then I would allow TV after they finish. I practiced mild discipline. I gave rewards when they did something good like received an award at school. I praise them for their work and caring. I also showed much love and care for them. The rules in my household were not difficult to follow. I reprimanded my children when they did something wrong. I let them know how disappointed I was with the negative behavior. I would always say, it hurts me as a parent to hear or see unruly behavior from you.

Whatever method you use, you are shaping your child in the direction of your teachings. And they will use your teachings for the upbringing of their children.

I am not going to tell you that I did not use negative behavior punishment. However negative discipline does not hold up. You want to think positively, and you will get a positive outcome.

RESEARCH ON RAISING CHILDREN

ACCORDING TO RESEARCH Human Development is a rich and varied subject. We all have personal experience with development, but it is sometimes difficult to understand how and why people grow and act as they do. "For example, why do children behave in certain ways?" Is their behavior related to their age, family relationships, or individual temperaments? The theories of child development explain various aspects of human growth.

I have had many years of experience working with children in early childhood education. I had many courses in child development in college. I relied on my educational experience of working in the classroom to raise my children. I have deep family roots from my mom in raising children, so I also followed the pattern of my mom pertaining to the growth and development of my children.

I followed the pattern of theorists like Piaget and Erikson in raising my children also. I admired those early child development pioneers. Erikson's psychosocial developmental theory is very interesting pertaining to early childhood and development throughout life. I appreciate the way he has put humans in eight stages from childhood to old age.

"Erikson's eight-stage theory of psychosocial development describes growth and changes throughout life, focusing on social interaction and conflicts that arise during different stages of development.

Next, I admired Piaget's cognitive development theory. His theory is concerned with the development of a person's thought processes. It also looks at how these thought processes influence how we understand and interact with the world.

Research has shown that high quality daycare is linked to cognitive development for disadvantaged children and many buffer against delayed language development when the quality of verbal interactions at home is low. In some cases, daycare may help narrow the achievement gap between privileged and under-privileged children. www.psychologytoday.com/us/blog/

ACCOMPLISHING MY GOALS

I WAS PHENOMENALLY successful at accomplishing my goals when I was growing up. I was responsible for all the talents and passions I created. In other words, with my mom special love and caring, I was able to move toward my future goals in a positive and happy way. I find it interesting that I have worked hard during my lifetime. I am a Baby Boomer. Baby Boomers are a generation of people who believe in working hard to succeed. However, bringing up my children from babies to adults, I never said you must work hard to succeed. I was an example of challenging work. They saw me working and continuing my education and being good at what I was doing. Be careful what you say and do because they are watching you. Most children grow up to become just like their parents. I know you are wondering and saying my child did not grow up to be like me. If you do the basic routine daily, then kids will follow you. Look closely and you will find yourself in your child or children.

Somethings that I like doing as an adult like teaching came from my mom. I love to teach. I used to watch my mom teach Sunday School. Later, when I was old enough, I started to teach younger children in Sunday School. After graduating from high school, I went to college. Later I started to teach Elementary School. I have three daughters who are successful teachers. They saw what I was doing and decided to teach, Then, two of my daughters married husbands who are teachers. I have one granddaughter who is a Speech Language Pathologist. Not all my family are teachers. Two children are in Health Care.

RAISING THE FIRST TWO CHILDREN

I RAISED SEVEN children. I got married at an incredibly young age. I was married to my first husband for 5 years before he passed away. After about 8 years, I remarried and had four more children with the second husband. I am telling you the story of raising seven children. My first marriage was short. He died so young. We had a wonderful time together with our two children. My first child was kindergarten age, and the second child was a baby when I lost my first husband. Mom moved in and helped me through my grief. She stayed with me an exceptionally long time. I had great support from my mom. With her support, I was able to return to work and college. After I married again, my mom was still living with us. My older two were in high school. My older two, who are girls were of immense help. They were babysitters for my children and helpers in my new business that I started, after graduating from college. I started a Child Development Center, which consisted of Preschool, Kindergarten, and Before and After school care. When my older two children graduated from high school, they went to college. They did not start a career in teaching. They went into different fields of study. Then, later they changed their minds and started a career in teaching. Four of the younger children became interested in Health Care. Only one of them became a teacher.

TAUGHT MY CHILDREN
TO LOVE AND CARE

ONE OF THE most important things to teach your children is to love and care. I told them that they must love each other. Sometimes, with siblings that can be challenging. If you want them to love and care for each other, then you should praise them when they are doing good. When you see them doing something like washing dishes and you did not ask them to do so, then praise them. You may compliment them by saying, I like the way you wash dishes. When I saw one of my children cleaning their room, I gave them a compliment because I was so glad that I did not have to clean it. I said, wow, you are doing an excellent job cleaning your room. Then, they started to clean their room more often. I kept praising them. And they all started to clean their rooms. I kept praising them until it became the norm. When your children do an excellent job at school, give your children a reward. There are thousands of children in our world today who do a good job in school and do not receive support or praise for their decent work. I gave my children a special treat when I saw a report card with good grades. I was looking at the news one day and was listening to a girl who said the audience praised her for the speech she gave in school on a science project. It was not the best speech ever, but her friends and family loved it. She received a huge hand clapping from the audience, and she continued her education in the field of science that she gave the speech in and now she is phenomenally successful in her career.

Now, I am thinking of a story from when I was in the eighth grade the teacher gave an assignment to do a news report. He explained what he wanted to see in the report. I went home and wrote my news report and got up in front of the class and said it. It was a great report. Watching the news with my mom, I heard the reporter say, I am bringing the news from the desert to the sea, to the mountains, and valleys, good evening. I am going to use this for my catch phrase, and it worked. I received 101 for reporting the news and I was overly excited. At that moment, I knew I was going to have a great life.

There are praises your children can get from you and their teacher at school or anyone in the community. I also praised my children when they played with each other in a wonderful way. When I saw positive play, I complimented them. I started early when they were little, then when they got to be teenagers, it was not so difficult to say, you must be nice to your sister or brother. If I had waited, then, it would be incredibly challenging for them because they would have already past childhood which encourages play. Play can be playing games together, outdoor activity or anything where children participate in a group.

When my children got older, the interest was in other friends. They forgot about the sibling play. They did share in adolescence, like clothes, jewelry, and games.

Next, I am thinking about discipline them when they are behaving negatively or breaking the rule. If that occurs, then start to talk about respect. If my children were not being respectful, then I would redirect them with positive behavior.

Finally, supporting your children's needs and ambitions are important. Sometimes my children would come to me with an idea or a desire to create something that they are very passionate about. I listened to what my children were thinking and if I thought there was some good in their creation, I gave full support. If you give your full support, then children do their best work. Some children are good at drawing. Some are great with making things using materials like wood, clay, playdough, and many other materials. Always listen to your children and give a helping hand when needed.

My teachings were to do good in school. I told my children to listen to the teacher and stay on task. Children listen to their parent advice. Even if you think they did not hear you, they do. Listening and staying on task are contributing factors to having success in school. However, there are other things that are just as important. You must apply the things that you learned to things and people around you. Also, your character traits play a key role in your success. My teachings were to be kind to others, share with others, always speak your opinion, and stay positive when others show negative vibes against you.

When children are at play sharing and being kind are significant factors in having good social skills. I told my children to try and always share your toys, games, or time with others. Share your time with a student who is sitting alone at recess or lunch. Sometimes when you start a conservation with that student you will find that the two of you enjoy the same things. Also, when you are on the playground near your favorite area to play in, like dodgeball, look around and ask someone to play who is also looking for an activity to do.

Another factor that contributes to doing well in school is doing your homework. I encouraged my children to always do their homework because it teaches responsibility. I believe in giving children homework because it helps to retain the lesson. If the homework refers to the lesson or lessons then it is good because it is a reteach or repeat of what you just learned in school, and it stays on your brains longer. And, if you do your homework, it sets you up for a successful future.

GOING TO CHURCH

ATTENDING CHURCH WAS important in raising my children. However, I was incredibly young with the first two, so I did not attend church regularly. Husbands from both marriages did not attend church. That had a profound effect on how we received religion. When my first born started to kindergarten, I went to church regularly because she was in a Catholic School. Later I changed my faith from Baptist to Catholic. The first two of my children attended Catholic school from kindergarten to 12th grade.

I do not remember my first husband attending church. The only time I do remember my first husband going to church was for the funeral of his sister. We both attended the funeral services and that is a time I remembered his church going. Although, it was a short marriage before he passed away, I was married to him for 5 years. He was in the Navy, so he would be at home for 6 months and at sea for 6 months. I cannot say he did not like going to church, but I did not go to church with him. For the second marriage, I remembered my husband attending church once also. That is when two of our children were baptized.

Trying to keep up with the tradition of attending church. The eldest two children went to church with my mom. When the eldest child started to kindergarten, we started going to Mass regularly and I changed from the Protestant religion to the Catholic religion.

The next generation of children I went to church regularly. Even though my husband did not attend church, I attended church. The second generation of children were able to attend church with my mom also. That is because I had to transport my mom to church on Sundays and then attend Mass in another location. Even though the older two of the second marriages had an opportunity to attend church regularly and continue in the Catholic faith, they choose not to.

For me when you choose a mate in life, you should be concerned about their religion. Make sure you are on the same page when it comes to religion. It makes for better communication regarding religion. I did not know so lesson learned. It made it difficult to explain religion to my children.

RESPECT OTHERS

TREAT OTHERS WITH kindness. I started early teaching my children to respect others. When they were growing up around two years old, I instilled in them to be kind to others. How can you explain or tell a two-year-old to respect others? One way of telling and showing them is to teach them to share. The two-year-old knows what belongs to him or her. If they are sitting next to another child and the other child sees them playing with their toy. Then, you may ask them to let the other child play or watch it for 5 seconds. You must tell them it is ok and hold the toy to let the other child play for 5 seconds. That method works sometimes. There are times when the child will not share because they are parallel playing anyway. Keep on practicing.

Next, I will teach them to respect others by speaking to them. Most young children do not say good morning, or good afternoon anymore. They walk or run past an adult or another child without speaking or even having to say sorry if they accidentally run into someone.

Think of the golden rule. Treat others with kindness, so why not treat others with kindness.

I told my children to always say Thank You when someone gives them a gift or do something nice to help them. Thank You and You are welcome are polite words that will stay with you forever. When you instruct children early in life, the above skills that I just talked about stay with them now and in the future.

Caring is another characteristic that they should have when giving respect to others. Be nice and respectful to people with disabilities and people who are less fortunate than you are.

GIVING

GIVE TO THOSE who are in need. Give to people who are less fortunate than you are. Give to the poor people. According to a song, the more you give, the more you receive. I have witness to giving and receiving the exact things that I gave. I received things that I needed and desired in abundance. Now, I love giving to those in need.

I taught my children to give to those in need. Now they are avid givers. Therefore, I said train a child while he is young to do certain charitable deeds. The most training they received in giving was watching me give to those in need. I carried them on a trip to a homeless place when they were around ages 10 and 12, and they helped me pass out food and drinks to the homeless. My children and I prepared things at home before we visited the homeless. My children helped me prepare the sandwiches, fruits, chips, and drinks to give to the people.

Another act of giving was birthdays parties that I gave for my children. I did not expect children to bring my children gifts, so I made party treat for everyone who attended the birthday party. I also provided food and entertainment. I also explained to my children that you do not have to receive a gift from family or friends. A birthday party is a celebration of your age, and you are happy and appreciate guests, friends, and family coming to your party. When you plan parties and say no gifts, come as you are then you are giving.

When my children grew up. They plan birthdays parties for their children and practice giving entertainment, food, and gifts to the guest.

When you think of giving, it is not always giving material things, I taught them to be available for others in need. For example, visiting the sick. We were in a church environment so during the Christmas Season, one way of giving was to go to Senior facilities and sing Christmas songs to the people who live there. My children also gave to the children who needed toys, games, and clothing.

CITIZENSHIP

CITIZENSHIP

BE A GOOD citizen. Follow the rules. You should listen for the first time. If your teacher or parent is giving a command listen and follow. When your teacher says to raise your hand in a classroom when you wish to speak, then do so. Remember, that is the rule in that teacher's class.

I explained Law Enforcement to my children, especially my boys. The law is unjust for Black lives. Even though the law is unfair, follow the rule and pray that nothing serious happens. When I say serious, the police officer shoots you. Then, you lose your life because you reached for your pocket when the officer said to put your hands up. Keep in mind, if you are stopped for a traffic violation it will cost you your life if you are not following the rules. Sometimes, when you have followed the rule, you may still lose your life. If the police pulled you over on a traffic violation, please follow the rules. Many Black people have been killed by the police officer because they shoot to kill instead of letting go of a simple situation like a busted taillight or no driver's license. We are still afraid of the Law enforcement today.

I taught my children basic rules, like do not drink and drive. Do not use your cell phone while driving.

Regarding fighting in any situation, use your words. Do not start a fight. However, if you need to defend yourself, then do.

WHEN I GROW UP

I WAS NOT a parent who told my children what you should do or become when you grow up. I did like to listen to them when they were talking about what I am going to do when I grow up. I used to listen to one saying I am going to be a doctor, then another would say I am going to be a nurse, then they would name a teacher, lawyer, engineer, and other careers. Then one of them said I am going to be rich, then I said what job are you going to work that will enable you to become rich. Then, they would reply that they could get rich in the jobs they just named. I also remembered having a preschool culmination exercise that focused on "When I Grow Up," was a topic that I was interested in learning about from preschool children and wanted to know at an early age what their thoughts were on adulthood. Most of them said Doctor, Nurse, Policewoman or Policeman, Fireman, or Fire Lady. I think one reason they name the latter fields is because they see these occupations a lot. So, they want to be like them. Many children in the lower economic group see the above occupations of police officer and police officer in a negative way. They see the officer in their community attending to a shooting or robbery. It would be nice if they could see them in a positive way. For example, helping the blind person cross the street or helping a lost child find their parent.

Children that are poor or in a different ethnicity group are watching the police stop someone in their car for a traffic violation or watch the police officer arrest someone for stealing in their community often.

I explained to my children that I respected what their goals were in life. I wanted very much for all of them to graduate from High School. They all graduated from High School. Four went to college and graduated from college.

Higher education is important for my family. The more knowledge you have allows you to understand the world we live in. With knowledge and understanding we can analyze our future goals and become more created and successful in them.

STAY HEALTHY

EVERYONE WANTS TO stay healthy. Most people are born with good health. However, it is up to us to stay healthy. When you were young your parents made sure you stayed in good health by caring for you. As you grew up your parents provided the best food, exercise, and wellness care for you. It was easy for me to provide the best care for my children when they were born until age ten. After they got older, they did not eat healthy food all the time. I worked full time when raising my seven children. I had to work full time to provide the necessities for my family. I cooked two or three days a week. I bought food already prepared from the grocery store. We also frequent fast-food places.

When my children became teenagers around age sixteen, they all wanted to work part time while in school. I signed permits for them to work after school 12 hours or less per week. They also contributed to eating fast foods and supermarket foods. It became difficult to eat healthily.

Food was not the only thing that contributed to staying healthy. My children were engaged in after school activities. For my boys it was football. The girls attended dance school. Two of my girls took music lessons. And one of the girls played a clarinet in the school band. One of the girls started singing. All the above contributed to a healthy, busy, and wholesome lifestyle. My first two children were engaged in music, dance, softball, and other school activities like student council. One of my older children ran in a contest and became the school queen.

My children got exercise growing up. We ate healthy food and some not so healthy foods. Now that I am older and they are all adults, I concentrate on telling the grandchildren to eat healthily.

WALK AWAY FROM TROUBLE

I TAUGHT THEM to walk away from trouble. My older son went with his friends to Magic Mountain. They were having a great time enjoying rides, eating good food and enjoying entertainment when a fight started among different groups of young people. The groups were throwing objects at each other and shouting insulting words at each other. That led to fighting individuals. My son and his friends became frightened and started to run away. They ran as fast as they could from the area. One of the friends was so frightened he climbed a tree. Finally, law enforcement can along and dispersed the crowd.

In the above situation, no one expected a fight at an amusement park. However, they were safe when they left the fighting area.

You should walk away from trouble. Sometimes you will have to defend yourself and cannot walk away. When someone is attacking you, then you must defend yourself. If someone hits you, then, you must defend yourself, sometimes you can say do not hit me again, and walk away. If the other person does not allow you to walk away then, you must fight back. When the person who started the fight in the first place sees you will be fighting back, they stop and run away.

FAMILY GATHERINGS

MY FAMILY LOVED holidays like Christmas and Thanksgiving. We also like celebrating birthdays and other holidays like Memorial Day, The 4th of July, and Labor Day. The latter holidays are low key because they occur at vacation time. Our family goes on vacation with their immediate family instead of extended family. Since I have seven adult children, they have family, and they vacation with their families.

We celebrate Thanksgiving and Christmas with a huge gathering. That is when all our families come together. There are 26 of us, but we have an attendance of around 20 per year. At Thanksgiving each family purchase food and cook their own food. They name the house where the celebration is going to take place. Then we all meet at that house and enjoy the great food and drinks. We have plenty of conservation and games to play. One of the favorite games for adults is Blackjack. We also watch the football games on Thanksgiving together for those who love football. The family discuss what they are grateful for and tell stories of what the future will bring for the family.

The future could be more travel, business opportunities, school, entertainment and many other points of interest.

At Christmas time, we celebrate big. We all agree the reason for the big celebration is the birth of Jesus Christ. We know the reason for our celebration because we believe in peace, joy, and love. These are the things Jesus Christ represents. We give gifts to each other, and we give gifts to organizations that help those in need. We play America's favorite game, White Elephant. The host also, gives a gift to everyone at the party. Our family is huge, so the host gives around 24 gifts. The gifts are usually household items and gift cards and cash. This year we had a family member donate several gifts for our White Elephant game.

When we celebrate, we give to others who are less fortunate. We believe in helping others that are in poverty. We also like to find new ways of educating people about being successful in today's world. My family today is like how I raised my children. The goal is to stay in school and stay focused. Stay on task in what you are trying to accomplish and listen to words of wisdom.

And last, all my adult children continue the things they were taught in celebrating birthdays with their own children. We believe in cake and ice cream and singing happy birthday until the child does not want it anymore.

They also traveled, went shopping, and to amusements places and did many of the same things that they did when growing up.

When my older two were incredibly young we traveled to many states and countries. Some of the places we visited were Hawaii, The Bahamas, Canada, and many states in the US. I was not aware at that time that kids would do the same thing, traveling when they became adults, today they have traveled many more places than we did.

My younger children and I traveled, but not as much as the older two. We were limited to places because I had five younger children, so we went to cities mostly in California. We went to San Diego, San Francisco, Sacramento and traveled to Las Vegas, NV a lot. We also went to Texas, Kansas, and Oklahoma. The younger children went to Hawaii also, but they were teens.

CULTURE AND ENTERTAINMENT

WHEN MY CHILDREN were young, we went to places like Disneyland, Magic Mountain and Knotts Berry Farm and many more places of entertainment.

This is one advantage of living in California and particularly Southern California because there are a lot of places to visit and a lot of things to do, like long walks on the beach or walking trails. When I lived in Los Angeles, my family and I frequently went to the beach. Having the Pacific Ocean in California provides opportunities for people to enjoy a lot of things near or on the beach. You can enjoy activities like boat riding, fishing, sightseeing, and many other amenities,

For my family, places of amusement brought out the excitement, adventure, and enjoyment to living our lives with joy.

We also visited the San Diego Zoo a lot because it was close to Los Angeles. The San Diego Zoo is huge and one of the largest zoos in the United States. We enjoyed looking at all the animals and birds and other mammals in the zoo. Then, I went to Sea World. I went there with the elder two. Long ago Sea World used to have a water show and boat ride. We loved watching the water show and riding on the boat. I returned to Sea World later when everyone had grown up and find a vastly different Sea World. Now Sea world is very crowded with many people. I barley saw very much, Although, there are plenty of new exhibits.

DAYCARE

MANY PEOPLE WOULD like to know how you managed to work and raise seven children. As I mentioned in the beginning, I had a lot of help from my mother in helping me raise my older two. However, the last five children I needed Daycare.

My elder two provided me with help taking care of my last five children. I could not use them all the time. They were in school too. I opened a Daycare. My Daycare consisted of a Pre School, Kindergarten, and Before and After care services for children ages 2-12 years. Three of my last 5 children benefitted from the Daycare. Times were hard and there was inflation. Parents were no longer able to pay for my services. I had only money enough to pay employees. I had to close and look for work elsewhere. I ended up going to a school district and applying for a teaching position.

I looked for a Daycare for my younger two children in my city. I found one. It was very expensive, but I managed to take my children there and continued my career. By the time I started working in the School District, the other three children were school age.

For a short time, the older three had to wait to be picked up by me after work. Later, they were able to ride the bus. Then after a couple of years we moved closer to the school, and they could walk. There were still some problems. My older son wanted to remain at the old school. He was in High School and determined to graduate with his classmates. He rode the school bus for a shorter time than the City Bus, and in his last year in High School, I was able to purchase a car for him. Daycare is more expensive now.

RESEARCH ON DAYCARE

RAISING SEVEN CHILDREN can be very stressful. There is hardly any time for self. Let's discover what the research says about Daycare. Does Daycare relieve some of the stress? "According to research the study of human development is a rich and varied subject". Research on Daycare talks about the expense of having to send your child or children to a service that provides a place to stay while you work is very expensive. They even explain how it is better to stay home because more than half of your income could be used for childcare fees. Then, some researchers focus on common childhood diseases that are found more often in children who attend Daycare than the children who stay home. The above may occur, parents still need to go to work.

There is some help for parents who have low or moderate income. With this help these parents can afford to send their children to daycare while working.

Regarding childhood diseases, maybe fewer common colds or flu but it also depends on the households. Some households have many family members.

There are many good things about sending your children to daycare, one being socialization. They will have that first opportunity of playing and interacting with others before going to school. Children that are at home without any outside contact with the environment will have a new experience with new friends other than family. Also, some Daycare Centers provide early childhood education which is very important before starting school.

There is no time for self.

Raising seven children can be stressful. There is hardly any time for self. How do you make time for self? I had to find out what do I like to do for relaxation and enjoyment. First, I like to sit in a comfy chair and just relax. I like closing my eyes and daydreaming. Then, after about five minutes, crab something to read like a book from my library or the newspaper or magazine. After reading one of my favorite books of self-help, I continued to sit for 5 minutes more. My next favorite thing to do for relaxation and enjoyment is shopping, I go to the shopping center and buy the things I need rather than go online and shop. When I was raising my children, there was not much shopping online. We went to the shopping malls or stores and bought goods.

I went on a trip alone while raising my children. This is the only trip I remember going on by myself when raising my children. I went to Las Vegas on a bus with other people. The people on this bus go to the casino strictly for gambling. This was a one-day trip which carried us to a hotel with a gambling casino. I remembered spending all day on the slot machines and eating at their restaurants.

After gambling and enjoying the food at the restaurants, we all boarded the bus for home. I do not remember any winnings. I did enjoy the trip.

As I stated above, raising children can be stressful if you do not have time for self. Also, you need the help of the other spouse. If you do not get minimal help it is very difficult raising children unless other family members are involved in helping you raised your children like grandparents. When both parents are working and you are using school time and daycare for support, that helps when you are working. However, when you get home, there is a whole new job awaiting you. So, unless you get that extra help, raising kids can be stressful and very tiring.

Many separations in families occur when there is not enough help in caring for children. To get a balance between husband and wife, they both must participate in childcare.

EFFECTIVE PARENTING STYLES

THERE ARE WHAT known as how to raise children or how effective are you in raising your children, I am referring to discipline, rules, family fun, emergencies and other family people which may be considered extended family.

Some parents are very strict when it comes to raising their children. An example of that would be demanding results from you children. If you do not make A's in school then I will not purchase that new bike for you. Another group of parents may see a large amount of freedom is good for their children. For example, They may allow children as young as 5 or 6 to let other kids come over when they are not around. Then, there are those who allow them to do whatever they see as right when things occur and they are not present to protect them I guess you can call it independent partening. for example, a child who is 9 or 10 should not talked to strangers, because they have been told not to both at home and school. However, when it happens, they hope the child will do the right thing, which is do not talk to strangers.

TODAY'S WORLD

IN TODAY'S WORLD there are some things that I think is very important. Please explain to your children about strangers. Tell them do not talk to strangers. Tell them if the unknown person tries and follow you when walking. Just keep walking. If there is a crowd, then get in the crowd and let someone know that you are being followed. If you have a phone call for help. Call home. Call 911.

However, always try and walk with another person especially when you are walking from school. Also, when you are going to the park, playground, or neighborhood market walk with another person.

CONCLUSION

RAISING CHILDREN IS not an easy task. There are many challenges when taking care of children. The parenting job encompasses a lot. There are so many tasks you must perform from birth to adulthood. Your newborn depends on you for nourishment, love, and care. For example, we must know when the baby is not feeling well. As the child becomes older, we are responsible for school, nutrition, play, extra curricula activities and other things like safety. On all the above we must try and make the right decision.

Next, bad things can happen even when you thought you taught them well. In school, at the park, at the market, and any place things can go wrong. For example, the child does not listen in school and becomes very disruptive and starts throwing objects that can hurt other students, the teacher, and perhaps themselves. That very incident is serious and causes serious consequences for that type of behavior. Next, even more serious problems where as your child committed a crime. This can be jail time or imprison.

There was a case like that just recently. the teenager went to school and shot four students. The teenager is in jail and the parents are also in jail. When you thought you brought your children up in the right way with good morals. You taught them what is right and what is wrong. Things can go wrong.

When children are introduced to the world around them it can shape a good part of their behavior. People environments consist of school, neighborhood, and other communities, and the entire town or city. Behavior is also influenced by television, computers, and a lot of technology.

The environment takes over. Whatever you thought you taught them goes out the window. The child own beliefs and morals may not be exactly the same always. The child can end up in jail or prison because of the negative things that were learned in the environment.

MENTAL OR PHYSICAL DISABILITIES

ANOTHER CHALLENGE FOR parents is raising children with mental or physical disabilities. That includes me. I did not raise my son with a mental disability, it happened when he turn seventeen years old. I will not discuss it now because I am including it in my next book in which I will talk about the mental illness in depth.

Parents with children that have mental or physical disabilities incur added responsibilities. Even though there is a lot of help from the community and your state or federal government taking care of children with disabilities is a huge task. Sometimes these children must attend special schools. And others may have a tremendous amount of hospital stay. The parents have huge daily tasks.

Most kids grow up like their parents. Most of your character traits are like your parents.

I had the experience of raising seven children. There were many challenges but also so many happy experiences from raising my seven children. I see that most of their character traits are like mine.

A CHALLENGE TO REMEMBER

IT IS NOT always positive when raising children. There are some things that happens which is beyond your control. For example, my last child is adopted. The Social Worker would visit my house at least every six weeks before the adoption became final. She visited on one occasion when my family and I had to move from a four-bedroom house to a two bedroom apartment. There were only two bedrooms so I had to be creative, because there was not enough sleeping space. I had bunk beds for the girls and boys. And, the baby which was around one year old had to sleep in our room in her crib. The Social Worker did not like the set-up. However, they did nothing to try and help accommodate us to live more comfortably. She went to the children's school and interviewed them for child abuse. She wanted them to say their parent spanked them. They did not volunteer any negative information. We successfully came out of that report because we were not abusive parents.

Children have committed crimes that led to killing people. However the case that I mentioned that just recently happened is the first time parents were arrested.

Many times the school, home, medical authorities, and other groups do not recognize the problem child. And, when they do, it is often difficult to know what to do to solve the negative or inappropriate behavior.

Most children grow up to be like their parents. They learn from you. Somethings may be inherited like singing, playing an instrument, public speaking, playing ball and many other talents but in general they watch their parents growing up and become like them.

Printed in the United States
by Baker & Taylor Publisher Services